US MILITARY

US NATIONAL GUARD

BY SUE GAGLIARDI

WWW.APEXEDITIONS.COM

Copyright © 2023 by Apex Editions, Mendota Heights, MN 55120. All rights reserved. No part of this book may be reproduced or utilized in any form or by any means without written permission from the publisher.

Apex is distributed by North Star Editions:
sales@northstareditions.com | 888-417-0195

Produced for Apex by Red Line Editorial.

Photographs ©: David J. Phillip/AP Images, cover; Shutterstock Images, 1, 4–5, 6–7, 8, 9, 10–11, 12–13, 15, 16–17, 18–19, 20–21, 22–23, 24, 26–27, 29; Garrett & Ruud/Library of Congress, 14–15

Library of Congress Control Number: 2022901409

ISBN
978-1-63738-314-8 (hardcover)
978-1-63738-350-6 (paperback)
978-1-63738-418-3 (ebook pdf)
978-1-63738-386-5 (hosted ebook)

Printed in the United States of America
Mankato, MN
082022

NOTE TO PARENTS AND EDUCATORS

Apex books are designed to build literacy skills in striving readers. Exciting, high-interest content attracts and holds readers' attention. The text is carefully leveled to allow students to achieve success quickly. Additional features, such as bolded glossary words for difficult terms, help build comprehension.

CHAPTER 1
TO THE RESCUE 4

CHAPTER 2
NATIONAL GUARD HISTORY 10

CHAPTER 3
HOW THE GUARD WORKS 16

CHAPTER 4
MANY MISSIONS 22

COMPREHENSION QUESTIONS • 28
GLOSSARY • 30
TO LEARN MORE • 31
ABOUT THE AUTHOR • 31
INDEX • 32

CHAPTER 1

TO THE RESCUE

A hurricane hits a city near the ocean. Many streets flood. Some people are trapped in their cars. Others are stuck at home. Many lose power.

Hurricanes can damage homes near the coast. Members of the National Guard may help clean up.

After Hurricane Sandy in 2012, the National Guard was called to help in 11 states.

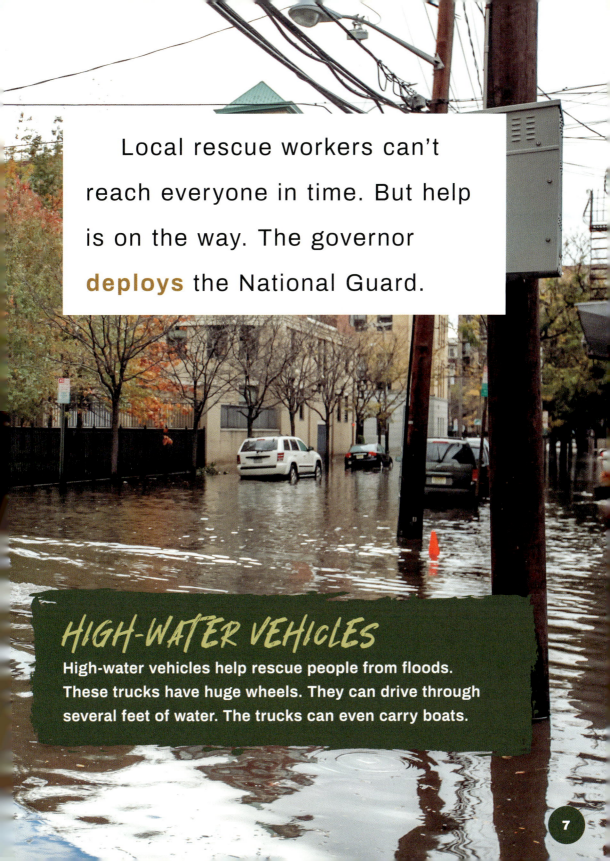

Local rescue workers can't reach everyone in time. But help is on the way. The governor **deploys** the National Guard.

HIGH-WATER VEHICLES

High-water vehicles help rescue people from floods. These trucks have huge wheels. They can drive through several feet of water. The trucks can even carry boats.

For some rescues, the National Guard uses helicopters. They lower long ropes to reach people.

Guard members arrive with boats and trucks. Some bring food and water. Others carry people to safety. Together, they save hundreds of people's lives.

◀ The National Guard often gives out supplies in places hit by bad storms.

CHAPTER 2

NATIONAL GUARD HISTORY

The National Guard is the oldest part of the US military. It was founded in 1636. Back then, the United States was not a country.

The first units in the National Guard formed in Massachusetts.

FAST FACT

Some members of early militias were called "minutemen." They could be ready to fight in a short time.

Instead, America was a group of **colonies**. The colonies formed **militias**. These groups fought to protect their communities.

People dress as members of an early militia in a parade honoring America's soldiers.

In the late 1700s, the colonies fought to be **independent**. Militias became part of the US military. In 1916, they were renamed the National Guard.

AIR AND ARMY

Today, the National Guard has two different parts. One is the Army National Guard. It is part of the US Army. The Air National Guard is part of the US Air Force.

Members of the Wisconsin National Guard served during World War I (1914–1918).

Soldiers in the Air National Guard fly many types of planes.

CHAPTER 3

HOW THE GUARD WORKS

E ach state has its own National Guard units. Some US **territories** have units, too.

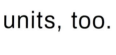

People often join their state's National Guard. But they can join a unit from another area.

National Guard members serve part-time. They attend several training sessions each year. The rest of the time, they have other jobs. But they can be called to **active duty** at any time.

Guard members train one weekend a month. They also have one longer training session each year.

CALLING THE GUARD

Each state's governor can deploy its National Guard. The US president can also call up the Guard. Guard members may help with a national emergency. Or they may be sent to another country.

People between ages 17 and 35 can join the National Guard. They must pass a **fitness** test. Then they go through basic training. They learn **combat** skills.

FAST FACT
In 2021, the National Guard had more than 430,000 members.

To prepare for combat, members of the National Guard learn to use rifles and other weapons.

CHAPTER 4

MANY MISSIONS

National Guard members protect their state and country. They are often sent to help local workers. They may help with rescues. Or they may help police.

Local workers and National Guard members often train together.

FIGHTING FIRES

California has many wildfires. The National Guard helps fight them. Guard members use helicopters to drop water on the flames. They also rescue hundreds of people and pets.

Guard members often respond to emergencies. They **evacuate** people from unsafe areas. They clean up after storms. They also help people get food or medical care.

In 2020, the COVID-19 virus spread very quickly. The Guard was called to help in many states.

Guard members may be deployed during conflicts, too. Some fight in wars. Others work to keep peace and order.

FAST FACT
The National Guard's motto is "Always Ready, Always There."

Guard members may provide protection for areas or events.

COMPREHENSION QUESTIONS

Write your answers on a separate piece of paper.

1. Write a sentence describing one job a National Guard member might do.

2. Would you consider joining the National Guard? Why or why not?

3. When was the National Guard founded?
    - **A.** 1636
    - **B.** 1916
    - **C.** 1947

4. Why do National Guard members have training throughout the year?
    - **A.** so they can serve full-time
    - **B.** so they don't have to travel
    - **C.** so their skills stay ready all the time

5. What does **respond** mean in this book?

Guard members often respond to emergencies. They evacuate people from unsafe areas.

    A. to stay quiet
    B. to take action
    C. to run away

6. What does **conflicts** mean in this book?

Guard members may be deployed during conflicts, too. Some fight in wars.

    A. times of peace
    B. times of fighting or trouble
    C. times when people stay home

Answer key on page 32.

GLOSSARY

active duty
Full-time work in the military.

colonies
Areas that are ruled by a different country.

combat
Fighting between armed forces.

deploys
Calls members of the military into action.

evacuate
To move away from a dangerous place.

fitness
The state of being strong and healthy.

independent
Not ruled or controlled by another country.

militias
Groups of people who are trained to fight, usually during times of emergency.

territories
Areas that aren't states but are still part of the United States.

TO LEARN MORE

BOOKS

Abdo, Kenny. *United States Army*. Minneapolis: Abdo Publishing, 2019.

Bassier, Emma. *Military Vehicles.* Minneapolis, Abdo Publishing, 2020.

Billings, Tanner. *The U.S. National Guard*. New York: Rosen Publishing, 2022.

ONLINE RESOURCES

Visit www.apexeditions.com to find links and resources related to this title.

ABOUT THE AUTHOR

Sue Gagliardi writes fiction, nonfiction, and poetry for children. She is a teacher and lives in Pennsylvania with her husband and son.

INDEX

A
active duty, 18
Air National Guard, 14
Army National Guard, 14

D
deploy, 7, 19, 26

E
emergencies, 19, 25

M
militias, 12–14
minutemen, 12
motto, 27

P
police, 22

R
rescues, 7, 22, 25

S
states, 16, 19, 22

T
training, 18, 20

W
wars, 26
wildfires, 25

ANSWER KEY:
1. Answers will vary; 2. Answers will vary; 3. A; 4. C; 5. B; 6. B